The Kid from Batley

Written by Brian Hewitt in 2018.
With additional chapter by daughters, Amanda and Sam.

First published on July 8th 2019 on the occasion of
Brian's 80th birthday.
Second edition published September 2023
Third edition published March 2025

Chapter 1

The Very First Years
1939 to 1954. Birth to fifteen years old

Brian at 7 months The back reads: 'Known as smiler. Do you wonder?'

I was born at 05.05am on 8th July, 1939, at 17 Laurel Grove, Wilton Estate, Batley, West Yorkshire. Obviously Adolf Hitler heard about me which is probably why he started the war. My parents were Lucy and Jack Hewitt and I was their third child, after Gerald (three years older) and Joan six years older). Tony came along eleven years after me.

I grew up going to Mount Tabor Sunday School and Carlinghow Junior School. I learned how to tap dance from about six years old and often played solo parts in my mother's pantomimes up to being about eleven. I learned my dancing at the Peggy Glenn Dancing School where I was the only boy dancer - in fact I was the only one in Batley! I also started piano lessons with Mr Arthur Dickinson when I was six.

We lived with rationing up to about 1957 or so, so I never tasted chicken until I was about seventeen! We basically lived on school lunches (9p for the week) as the main meal of the day, and then a slice of jam and bread for tea. Our big treat was rabbit stew at the weekend.

The earliest things I remember (just) is going into our cellar when the bombing was supposed to be going on. Sometimes we just hid under the table, whereas Grandma James used to just go to bed saying she would rather die there than in the cellar.

Life was basically run by Grandma since Dad was in foreign parts in the Army and Mother worked in Taylors weaving mill from 7.30am to 5.30pm every day, and then as an usherette at the Princes Cinema in Birstall in the evenings. My father finally came home from five years overseas (Egypt) on the 15th August 1944. It was the first time I ever saw him - I think that was why he was always a bit of a stranger to us as we were growing up.

Me with Grandma James, about age 4. She was knock-kneed and I was trying to stand like her.

Grandma used to cook on a stove which was part of the fireplace in the kitchen and which also had sort of grill to put pans on. We didn't have a cooker.

On the domestic front we didn't have a washer either so washing was done by hand in a big metal 'peggy' tub in which the clothes were placed in hot water, and then we had a scrubbing board on which we (mostly Grandma) scrubbed all the clothes until clean (hopefully).

When I got a little bit older - say 5/7 or so - Grandma, who was forever going to the doctors, used to take me with her and then to the pictures (cinema) - Low Lane Cinema in Birstall.

Life at 17 Laurel Grove in Batley was quite a close-knit community thing with all the other kids from the houses around us. Wilton Estate was our world in those days. I remember some of the other kids names - Raymond Milnes, Maureen Woollin, Margaret Eatough, Jack Eatough, and Terry and Peter Mann our next door neighbours - and we used to always play *Hide and Seek* - we used the gas-lamp to lean on when we were counting to 100 before going in search of the hiders. Talking of gas lamps, I find it amazing that in the 1940s a man used to come round the estate every evening to light all the gas lamps, and then return in the morning to put them out. We played other games all the time including *Hopscotch* and *marbles* in a series of holes which we dug in the grass patch in front of our house. Marbles and ball-bearings had a value depending on their size. Strange! One big bearing was worth six small ones and we actually used to trade these between ourselves as though it was money.

August 1950, age 11.

There was one special little moment at Carlinghow School which only I know about. It was a moment when I realised how to make money easily. The plan I had was to simply find a way to get everyone in the country to give me one penny (*which no one would ever miss*) and that would make me thousands of pounds! I have since been referred to as ***the penny in the playground kid.*** When you think about it, it is the way the world works today - just small amounts from lots of people.

This little community remained very close knit up until I was about eleven and included regular outings to the park just across the road. We used to row the boats, climb the trees in the woods and play on the swings and roundabouts. When we were a bit older, we used to do putting and bowls with some of the boys. The park also had a bandstand where we could listen to brass bands playing. Tennis came later at eleven, mainly because my eldest brother, Gerald, started with his pals and I tagged along. It is only on looking back that I realize just how lucky we were to have the park there to entertain us. We were there nearly every day. It was wonderful – and, amazingly, it still is.

When the day was over in the park we used to then go across the road to Albert Graham's fish and chip shop to have two pennyworth of chips with 'bits' (scraps of batter that came off the fish). There is actually a fish shop today in Huddersfield call Wi' Bits.

Another important element of this period included (of course) lots of trips to Morecambe. It really was a big part of life back then for Joan, Gerry and me. We used to play on the sands all week and then - only on the Friday before we came home - we were allowed to have a ride on the Cyclone (big dipper) and on the horses on the sands. Both cost a shilling.

Mother used to take me on what she called 'Mystery Trips' on the local bus service on Sunday afternoons. They weren't that mysterious as we always went to Wetherby for fish and chips.

I started schooling at a nursery in Carlinghow when I was about

four and we used to go to bed every afternoon on little cots. My blanket had a yellow duck on it and I made a card for mother where I copied that duck. It still exists somewhere!

According to my mother's diary, I started at Carlinghow Junior School along with my playmates from Laurel Grove when I was six which was presumably a bit later than usual due to the war. My early teacher, Miss Danvers, used to come and see me in mother's pantomimes doing my song and dance act. It was at Carlinghow that I first met Christine Exley (later Horne) as we were in the same class even though she was a year younger (she was a clever beggar so got moved up a class). She was not only clever but posh too as the family owned Exley's Shay Farm on Bradford Road. They had apple trees with branches growing over the wall so we used to pinch their apples. Until she sadly died, we saw a lot of her and her husband Doug as they lived close by. Christine bought us an apple tree when we lived in Durham so she could pinch *our* apples! We still have it.

One of my roles at school was to walk round the whole school ringing a big bell at the end of the lunch break to tell all the kids to go back to the classrooms. As I was doing this I could see my mother hanging out of a window of a hospital up a hill (where she worked for while) waving a duster at me.

We couldn't afford sweets at school but we did go to what we called the *Top Shop* just up the road from school to buy Oxo cubes for one old penny. These we just licked to bits. I still like Oxo drinks made with hot water.

Gerry was at the same school at this time but I think we used to just have our own pals that we played with due to the three year age gap. We also used to go home after school with our pals as well. I don't remember going home with Gerry at all, but I do remember going to one of Batley's four cinemas (Plaza, Regent, Empire Super and the Victoria) to see Roy Rogers and Gene Autry cowboy movies. A bit later I remember going with friend to the Gaiety in Batley every Saturday afternoon. We used to dance with girls who were let in free of charge so they'd get the boys up to dance. That was where we learned to bop to music like Rock Around the Clock.

My younger brother, Tony, was born at 11.30 on 16th June 1950 and by August 1954 we had to move to a bigger council house round the corner at 4, Ealing Crescent. Then Joan left us to start a new life in Canada, sailing on the *Empress of France* from Liverpool on 4th June 1954. She went to stay with one of mother's friends who'd gone there three years earlier: Aunty Dorothy. Then in 1956, Gerry was called up for National Service in the Air Force on 7th Feb 1956. All this meant we had to downsize our house again to reduce rent, so we moved to nearby 5, The Bower.

When it came to 11-plus time, my mother told me not to worry and keep telling myself that *I WOULD PASS!* So that is presumably what I did instead of working and so I failed the exam and lost the chance to go to Grammar School. My teacher, Miss Rhodes, was very distressed about it and called me in to tell me that she couldn't believe it. Later at Healey Secondary Modern I was given the chance to go directly to the Grammar School since I was top of the class. But Gerry had told me that the kids who did that never caught up and so not to do it. So, despite both mother and father going to Healey to see the Headmaster, I refused and stayed where I was. Crackpot!

One big moment at Healey Modern was being given a 10 out of 10 for an essay by Mr Schofield who said that it was the only 10 he had ever given to anyone and thought it would remain the only one. Quite on pat on the back.

It was whilst at Healey that I went to Pateley Bridge to the Bewerley Park School for a month on the 23rd June 1952. It was absolutely wonderful and the memory has remained with me for the rest of my life. It is a place I still have to visit even now.

I also ended up becoming the School Captain (as we were called rather than Head Boy) so at least I did the best I could without the Grammar School background.

During the period 1952 to 1954, I did a paper round six days a week straight after school for 7/6p per week (about 37 pence today). The paper round started from a shop in Carlinghow and I did the whole of Wilton Estate in about one hour. I used to spend some of the money on sweets but they were rationed back then following the war.

As my final school year was coming to a close, we were all taken to visit places like coal mines and weaving mills (including one called Dewhursts in Batley Carr, which is now called Redbrick and I visit quite regularly for coffee). All these places of work needed people badly following the war. Not that any of them interested me much (they were too dirty for me) but I still had no idea of what I might do for a job. I left school on the 23rd July 1954.

Chapter 2

Senior School and the early Slazenger Period
1954 to 1959. Age fifteen to twenty

I was possibly the best junior tennis player in Batley and district by the time I was fifteen. I played with a Slazenger tennis racket, but I didn't know that the Slazenger factory was just a little way off in Horbury near Wakefield. It was Gerry that found this out and suggested it was worth a try for a job. Bear in mind that, in those days, no-one had a car and the only places that we knew were Batley, Dewsbury and Leeds. There were no direct bus services to anywhere else that we knew at that time, so Wakefield was like the end of the world.

My mother picked up on this somehow arranged an interview with the personnel manager and took me there for the interview. Not that we ever knew about it at the time, but with the war just nicely over there was a huge shortage of people to do all the jobs that were available and so the employers were always on the lookout for new people. I was interviewed by three heads of departments: tennis racket manufacturing, cricket bat manufacturing, and then the chief accountant since they were always short of clerks apparently.

I decided on the office job on the basis that it started at 8.30am rather than the factory which started at 7.30. I already had a long journey to get there and still had to leave home just after 6.30am to get there on time. I started on 9th August 1954. Slazenger was probably the best sports company in the world at that time with branches overseas as well as in the UK. The factory is still standing although now filled with a lot of different businesses. In those days it was amazing, with over a thousand people working there making an incredible range of sports goods: rackets for tennis, squash, badminton, table tennis, cricket, rounders; archery bows and arrows; golf clubs and balls; tennis balls, footballs, rugby balls; cricket gloves and wicket keepers gloves . . . the list was endless.

March 1955. Working in Slazenger's wages department.

My first job at Slazenger was in the leather costings department where all I did was collect the workers clocking-in cards for the tannery department and work out how many hours they had all done and so how much they got paid. That lasted about six months, after which I went to the Wages Department, where I helped with the planning for wages day on Thursday and went round with trays full of wage packets for the workers. Imagine people nowadays joining a big queue to collect their weekly wages from a young kid!

This probably went on for a period of about a year or so, after which I did a period in the General Office working out the royalty payments for our sports stars like Len Hutton, Don Bradman, Fred Perry (who I was later to meet at Wimbledon). After that, I was transferred to the Wood Costings office doing heaven knows what.

Finally, I was moved to the Sales Department to answer the phone to shops placing orders and run the internal shop where, every Thursday, employees could buy cheap items deemed unfit for sale.

Those Slazenger years were terrific and during the summer I sometimes went to work on my bike which made a change.

During the breaks and at lunch time we all used to play table tennis and snooker in a rest room above the main canteen. Also, we had a couple of people in the offices who played for Wakefield Trinity (rugby league), a game I loved watching.

My time at Slazenger also provided me with a life-long friend, Arnold Robinson. He was nine years older than me and worked in the wood costings office. We remained friends until he died on July 9th 2022. I miss him badly.

Outside of work, I re-started my tap-dancing on the 28th October 1955 and, being the only male dancer in Batley, I got to do solo dances in the shows which were put on by the teacher, Peggy Glenn. I badly wanted to be Fred Astaire so tap was my focus but I also did some ballet to improve posture, and American Stage Dancing where you fly about and slide on your knees.

I started with Dewsbury Collegians along with mother 18th September 1956 and took part in *Call Me Madam*. My first show with Batley was in October 1957 - White Horse Inn. It was at this time I met another lifelong friend, Noel Rigg and his brother Dennis. Noel was to marry Dorothy and they are still my best friends. (Sadly Noel died in August 2023).

I started my elocution lessons on 28th October 1956 with a famous man in Batley called Whittaker, a really scary Shakespearean actor who was the teacher of film star Donald Pleasence known for playing Blofeld in a James Bond film, *You Only Live Twice*. Part of the training included saying, 'Arround the rrough and rrugged rrocks the rragged rrascal rran'.

At this time, I also did a night school course in Dewsbury to learn typing and shorthand. I never mastered shorthand but could do about forty words a minute typing which was fairly good.

The only photo of the whole family. Gerry, Joan, Brian, Tony, Lucy, Jack. About 1954.

Our Grandma, who brought us all up, went into Oakwell Geriatric Hospital near Birstall. She couldn't walk anymore. Since my sister, Joan, was in Canada by now and Gerry had just been called up for National Service, I was the only one - apart from Mother - who went to visit her. I sometimes used to set off to the pictures and whilst waiting for the 'A' bus to take me to Batley or Dewsbury, a special hospital bus used to come the other way so I would cross the road and go and see Grandma instead. I used to do that a lot. She died in 1967 at 92 years of age, but amazingly, she outlasted our Dad, who died a year earlier in 1966, aged only 58.

During these early teen years, Gerry and I used to go to St John's Church at Carlinghow (mainly so we could go to the youth group with our pals). The church had its own Amateur Operatic Society and this led us to being in an amateur show called *The Girlfriend* - less famous than the later *Boyfriend*. We also used to go to old time dancing on Friday nights. So, the church was central to our universe.

At eighteen, I won the Batley Junior Tennis Championship! I also got to the final of the Huddersfield singles later that year.

On the 6th December 1957, I (stupidly) left Slazenger and went to London with a huge suitcase expecting to become a film star or something.

Batley Junior Tennis Champion, 1958

It took me two days of going to all the theatres and asking for jobs only to realise it wasn't going to happen. How anyone could think of trying that in December is incredible. I could certainly have hacked it in show business as I could actually do the stuff required, but I just had no idea how to go about it.

I went back on hands and knees and begged for the job back at Slazenger. I took a lot of ribbing and, oddly, the chief accountant, David Barnes, told me I should have asked him as he knew a famous entrepreneur called Val Parnell and he could have introduced me and got me into show business with no trouble!

17 years old. A film star in the making!

Slazenger Christmas party 1958

At eighteen going on nineteen, I was to star in *Oklahoma* as Will Parker in Batley Amateurs, alongside Jean Terry (now President of Dewsbury Collegians). Jean turned out to be the biggest star of amateur theatre – perhaps in the country – as she starred in over 60 productions for various companies in the region. She was outstanding, though modest.

About this time, I got a girlfriend called Jennifer Keighley and we kept going until I went in the Army during which time I came home on leave and finished it. Much to her dismay. (*Very sadly she was to die very shortly afterwards in 1968, aged only 25*).

Chapter 3

National Service to Breakfast at Tiffany's
1960 to 1961. Age twenty-one to twenty-two

I left Slazenger again in January 1960 as I had to do National Service in the Army. I started in Catterick on the 7th January at 8th Signal Squadron as Signalman Hewitt 23757189 (you never forget your army number). I was one of the very last boys ever called up as the system was stopped just after I went in. I was disappointed at the time but in the end had a really great time

Basic training at Catterick Camp, January 1960

and wouldn't have missed for the world.
On the morning I joined up, I had to catch a bus to Batley, then walk to the station for a train to Darlington. On the train I met another boy who was joining up and we ended up in the same

group together. In Darlington, we changed train to Richmond, where we were met and put in an army truck and driven to the Royal Signals Army Camp. There, we were all put in a line with our arms bare and injected in both arms by people on either side of us.

Basic training simply involved living in a tin hut and being got up early and then having to learn to march properly with the other lads over a four-week period. After that we got about a week off to go home and then re-started back at Catterick at 24th Signal Regiment in different barracks, which were a bit more civilized. This period was called 'Trade Training'.

Outside my house in Cyprus June 1960. 'I'm not half as happy as I look.'

I was put on a course to be a clerk (even though I had my Slazenger experience behind me) so spent the time typing and doing little else except play rugby and do a bit more marching and drink tea in the NAAFI.

After about eight weeks of this, we were asked our preference in terms of postings. So, I asked for the Far East as it was apparently very good. However, the hostilities were just coming to an end in Cyprus between the Turkish EOKA terrorists and the Greek majority. It was still a bit tense when we got there, and we lived in tents (roof only with open sides since the temperatures were very high) and we lived behind a fence and could only go out to Nicosia in groups. We did get to go to Kyrenia most weekends in a truck and had a great time swimming off the rocks there. I had my 21ˢᵗ birthday in camp there, which was made all the more special by being put on Guard Duty all night.

My job was movements clerk, which meant that I had to arrange everything for anyone being moved to another regiment or country. So, no great surprise then that I got very busy around September 1960 when peace was signed between the Turks and Greeks, and our 51ˢᵗ Squadron was to be abandoned.

I set about arranging for all the 200 or so men to be posted elsewhere and even got mentioned dispatches for the long hours I put in. When we got down to the last few, we quit the camp and moved the last half dozen or so into a hotel in Nicosia. We finally ended up with just a captain and me who were both going to 234 Signal Squadron in Malta. We finally went to the airport to get the flight but when we got on the plane the captain got a seat and I was left with no seat and so had to get off the plane.

> wheels going on our few remaining vehicles during the last critical days of the run-down.
> The man with the biggest task in the unit was Lance-Corporal Hewitt, the Movements Clerk. All personnel moving from the unit passed through his capable hands and many an evening saw the midnight oil being burned to ensure that everything was completed for each draft's movement. But trying to work out what the other eight clerks in R.H.Q. did was a difficult task until one remembered the chap who brought the Coca-Cola and the clerk who kept the Adjutant's (Captain J. Mills) pencils sharpened.
> The task of administrating, feeding and accommodating about 150 men while the roofs were literally torn from above their heads was a problem well taken care of by H.Q. Squadron, commanded by Captain P. Wetherill. On 19th August, 1960,

Snippet from the Batley News in 1960 when the camp at Nicosia was closed.

With no plan in place I called a sergeant that I knew at the other side of the island in Episkopi. He sent a jeep for me and brought me to his camp where I just parked in a tent on my own on the side of a hill looking out to sea. It took nearly a month for them to get me on a flight and I just had a great time swimming and going to the canteen for meals and collecting my pay packet on Thursdays.

Finally, a flight came through on 19ᵗʰ October 1960 and I was whisked off to Malta to spend one of the best periods of my life.

It was fabulous just doing a bit of office work from 8am until 1pm and then going off to Sliema to spend the afternoons in the sea. While I was there, a new version of the New Testament Bible came out so I decided to try and understand religion a bit better by reading it. I read it twice and still don't know how it works. However, my tennis playing became known and I was soon in the Army team which was to win the Inter-Services cup against the Air Force and Navy without dropping a single set. This made the papers in Batley. *Yes, that famous!*

Hard-working clerk in Malta. October 1960 to December 1961.

But this is what I mostly did in Malta!

I did one sensible thing in Malta and that was to go to night school once a week and take an O-level in English (I passed!). It was there that I actually got a great accolade by virtue of the fact that the teacher, an army sergeant, gave us an essay to do and when we went back the following week, he passed the marked papers back to the other guys but when he got to me he threw it down and said, 'I'm not marking that as you copied it from a short story book.' I didn't know what to say, so I said nothing. How could I prove I did it myself? In the end I just took it as a great compliment and left it at that.

The story was only a couple of pages long and was about a church service being held for a little girl who was dying and couldn't be saved by the medics. The family and friends took her to the church where the vicar held a special service for her and asking God for her to be spared. When the service was starting, no-one noticed a young boy coming in to sit alone at the back of the church. As the service was drawing to a close, the little girl suddenly stood up all smiling and happy, obviously completely recovered! All the family and friends were ecstatic and crying with joy all around her, but what no one noticed at all was that the little boy sitting quietly at the back of the church had the small glow of a halo above his head!

A daily part of life in Malta was that, after eating dinner about 5.30 in the barrack's canteen, we use to go up to Valetta which was only about five minutes from our base in Floreana. The main street (Republic Street) was always very busy with locals walking up and down it all night chatting to friends. We used to do the same.

It was in July 1961 that I got leave to come home for Gerry's wedding to Jean Townsend. Mother and I also made time to visit the theatre to see My Fair Lady.

I was a bit worried that someone would have got my good job in the sales department in Horbury, I wrote to Buzzer Hadingham - the big Slazenger boss who I had never met - and asked for an interview with a view to getting back into the sales department rather that the general office after demob. The meeting went better than I could have ever dreamed of and when I got back to Malta after the wedding, a letter came from Buzzer offering me a job as the Area Sales Manager (basically a sales rep). This meant having a car which I had also never dreamed of. Heaven on wheels!

    No-one had ever been promoted out of the factory onto the road as a salesman before. I should say at this point, though, that my younger brother Tony started Batley Grammar School this year. He was so much smarter than me.

So, I enjoyed my last few months in Malta very much and when I finally came close to my demob date, I discovered that there was a special arrangement available which entailed getting out a month earlier by paying for my own flight home. So, instead of going back to Catterick to be demobbed on the 7th January 1962, I got a local release right there in Malta on the 7th December 1961. This meant that I got home for Christmas and also made it to the annual sales conference with the big management and the other salesmen in mid-December 1961. It's

impossible to convey how good it felt to be doing that after just being an office boy before going into the army. One of the great people I met at that conference was John Barrett, a great tennis player who became the Davis Cup Captain. He subsequently wrote the Wimbledon Record Book which is updated by him every year and he was also the chief BBC commentator on The Championships at Wimbledon for twenty-five years. I speak to him occasionally and he kindly invited Arnold Robinson and I to Wimbledon from time to time.

The best thing by far, of course, was that getting home before Christmas saw me invited by a friend from the Collegians - Barry Senior - to a pantomime in which he played the Dame. He also invited to go along at the same time in the next seats, two young ladies: Joy Airey, who I knew from the Amateurs, and another young lady I didn't know called Valerie Windrow. At the end of the show, Valerie and I walked in the same direction for a bus - hers going one way to Thornhill and mine going the other to Batley. Before parting, we had arranged a date to go and see *Breakfast at Tiffany's* which, according to my mother's diary, we did on the 4th January 1962. That film and the wonderful song, *Moon River*, was to follow us throughout our life together. *Moon River* is our song.

So, the die was cast and was the best thing that ever happened to me … and some.

It was the end of one great period and the start of another.

Chapter 4
Just Married

1962 to 1969

After our first date I took Valerie home to Island View on the outskirts of Dewsbury and there, memorably, we had our first kiss standing on a patch of grass at the end of the track into Island View. A moment I never ever forget.

Fortunately, Valerie had a scooter and her father Harry (later to be named Poppop by my girls, Amanda and Sam) drove me home on the back of it as it would have been quite a walk to Batley.

I spent the next two months or so going around the sports shops in the area that I was to become sales manager of. This was with the incumbent Bill Greenwood who was showing me the ropes. In those days there were only about a seventh of the cars we have on the road today, so driving was a lot easier. My area was from Morecambe in the west across country to Harrogate and then across to Bridlington in the east and all the way up to the Scottish border.

The job of travelling salesman was completely ideal for me as I was good communicating with people. Generally, I was in Newcastle every week as that was the richest patch I had and then the rest of the time I arranged trips around the area which usually included four or five calls per day. Amazing to think that in those days there were about three thousand sports shops in the UK and today that number is only about four hundred. How things have changed. So every couple of months or so I started by going to Hexham where there was one sports shop and then on to Haltwhistle for the next and then to Carlisle where there were three shops. Before arriving there, though, I called on the Carlisle Golf Club as they were also part of the job. I usually stayed in Carlisle over night before driving down to Workington and Whitehaven to a shop in each town plus the golf clubs. I then ended the trip in Barrow and Ulverston before travelling round to Morecambe to stay the night there before setting off on the return journey via Kendal, Cockermouth and Keswick where I also stayed the night before heading home the next day. I did the same thing on the east coast as well with the same sort of routine. One interesting thing about staying in hotels in those days was that you always left your shoes outside the bedroom door and someone would clean them during the night. If you did that today they would be pinched before you got up.

We had two major sales efforts each year - one for the summer season (tennis rackets, cricket bats etc) which we did from about October until March, and then the winter season from about April to September. At the start of each selling season we held what were called *Stock Rooms* where we set up displays of our samples in a hotel and the retailers who were near enough would come and visit us and place the orders there. These we held in the Royal Turks Head in Newcastle and another in Manchester and yet another in the Albion Hotel in Leeds. These were always attended by our Sales Manager, Charlie Colcutt, from Head Office. One night when I was in the restaurant in the Turk's Head Hotel, I was shocked to see that the only two other people in there were Cilla Black and Bobby Willis!

During this time, I was home every weekend of course and went out with Valerie to both the cinema and to the Majestic Ballroom in Leeds where we danced to the live bands after eating at a restaurant first. Amazingly, we felt pretty rich on my salary of £750 a year plus expenses. Within a few weeks, Slazenger gave me my first car - a Ford Consul, reg number RVH38 - and so Valerie and I were well set up. During this time she was still working as a Dental Nurse in Ossett.

At the end of March 1962, I was going to live during the week in Durham at the Public School there in a lovely old house called Old Caffinites with Mr and Mrs John Hall. He was the senior science master and they were a lovely couple. This happened because the school had a Slazenger account which meant that they were my customers. The shop was in a part of Caffinites and the manager told me about the flat next door and introduced me to the Halls. A lucky break!

Maybe thinking that I was about to vanish up north, Valerie took things in hand (as she would) and proposed to me on the 31st March. Thank God! I duly bought her an engagement ring in a shop in Dewsbury (cost a fortune I'm sure, probably about £7.00!)

I continued coming back to Batley/Dewsbury each weekend to be with Valerie as we started to plan our marriage. I remember she bought her wedding dress in a Leeds shop for about £15.00.

Valerie made a trip to Durham with me and stayed at Old Caffinites so that we could look around for a house to buy.

We did consider other places such as Ripon but decided that Durham looked favourite.

Eventually, we found a semi-detached house in Gilesgate Moor at 24, Moor Crescent and paid the mighty sum of £2,400 for it.

We did quite a lot of get-togethers between her parents, Harry and Mattie, and my mother and father. We also visited Auntie Betty and Uncle Jack and children Gillian and Nigel and other aunties and uncles on their side. I didn't have much going on in terms of relatives apart from Tony since Joan and Gerald (my older siblings) were off in Canada. Joan had gone on 4th June 1954, and Gerald and Jean had gone on the 9th August 1961 after they married.

So, finally we arrive at the 2nd March 1963 at Thornhill Church where we got married, and then Marmaville Country Club in Mirfield for the reception. It was wonderful, then we drove off from Island View to Blackpool for our honeymoon.

The restaurant where we had dinner on the first night is still there and we stayed at the big Imperial Hotel, but only for one night as we were dying to get back to our new house in Durham.

So, we went straight home the next day to see both parents in Batley and Dewsbury, then left immediately to start life in our new home in Durham. Whoopee!

We didn't have all the furniture we needed, but we made do in the living room by staining the floor brown and then buying a sheep fleece to put in front of the fire. The fleece cost £9.00 which we got by selling Harry a £10 lot of premium bonds (which he had given us in the first place).

The stair steps were covered with little pads of cloth since we couldn't afford carpets at that time. We also got our first telephone, which was a party line shared with next door. Hardly anyone had a phone in those days. Most people just went to the nearest phone box and put in four pennies to make a call. You had to book overseas calls in advance!

Valerie was straight into the domestic scene while I had to go back to work travelling and being away pretty much two nights

24

every week. She was great at everything and also took up gardening as well.

We must have been careless as ten months later Amanda Gale was born on 15th January 1964. Valerie actually had the birth pains starting while we were in Dewsbury doing our usual visits, so we raced back home and got there nicely in time so that Amanda arrived in Durham's Dryburn Hospital. We never slept a wink for two years! Amanda's middle name was spelled Gale because of a lady in a TV series called the Avengers - played by Honor Blackman who crops up again later. I used to walk around with Amanda half the night and then after putting back in her cot I would try and creep out and back to bed but she always stood up a cried as I reached the door.

Harry and Mattie used to come up and see us a lot (I would make a trip to Slazenger and then pick them up and bring them back). Harry then got into a routine of taking Amanda out in the pram for walks down by the Tin School, down Dragonville Lane.

Time passed by doing our thing of bringing up Amanda and earning a living etc. We had no particular friends at this time apart from Mr and Mrs Hall at the school, but that was to change in due course.

And then of course came big trouble in the shape of Samantha Louise who arrived at home in Moor Crescent on the 25th November 1966. While the midwife was helping Valerie with the delivery I was waiting on the bottom bedroom step for sounds of screaming. When they finally came, however, I was knocked to one side by Mattie who nearly trampled me to death in order to get to see the baby before me. I finally got to see Sam, but only after Mattie.

That arrival had a few blessings in the shape of her being a very good sleeper and no trouble. Also we used the pending arrival to tell Amanda (who never slept all night ever) that she had a baby sister or brother coming and that she would have to go into a big bed and would have to go to sleep so as not to disturb the new baby. It worked; we never heard another squeak out of her.

On the work front I had made my first contact with a film star in the form of Honor Blackman who played Pussy Galore in *Goldfinger*. (And Mrs Gale in *The Avengers* - mentioned above).

Buzzer Hadingham apparently knew Cubby Broccoli who was the producer of James Bond films and when the film was released in late 1964, he managed to get Slazenger mentioned in the film during a golf scene. Because of that, when Honor Blackman visited Newcastle Odeon to publicise the film at the Premier, I managed to get myself invited by the manager of the cinema and then also managed to get a photograph with her which went viral within the sporting media of the time. Nice picture.

During this same period (1964/65), Slazenger set up the McDonald sales incentive scheme for the sale force by offering us points for all the sales we made over certain the targets they set for us. Needless to say, I wiped the floor with everybody in this and made enough money to completely refurnish our kitchen and buy a new Hoover Keymatic washing machine. We actually had enough points to buy Valerie a mink fur coat which was listed in the catalogue, but she took the sensible approach and fitted the kitchen instead.

The nearest competitor to me got something like a dozen hankies. So, I was not all that popular with the rest of the sales team, especially one of them who later became the Sales Manager and was very much the reason why I had to leave Slazenger in due course. I remain certain that he was the reason and it was just jealousy.

On that subject, I got permission from the then sales manager to open a sports shop in Bishop Auckland. It was this that the new sales manager went after me for and said I couldn't be a competitor to my customers and a salesman. It just so happened that two of the other sales guys also had shops as well but he didn't say anything to them. I always thought that if I had stayed at Slazenger I would have ended up running Wimbledon or something.

The mid-sixties were pretty lively with playing tennis for Ashbrook (Sunderland) Club with all the county boys and I also did my year of learning aikido and got to blue belt standard (two below black belt) so not too bad. When I showed Valerie my new moves she always beat me up, so aikido was no good against her.

It was also a good time for famous people as I somehow got to know the Barron Knights who were a famous group who imitated other top line groups of the day. I used to play squash and golf with them, especially a guy called Pete Langford (known as Peanuts). I spoke to him on the phone last year; he is now managing other artists.

The other stage people I knew well were the Black and White Minstrels. I used to play golf with one of the lead guys when they were touring. I actually took both groups on tours of Slazenger which of course went down well with all the workers. There were a lot of the Minstrels with dancers so they arrived as a bus load.

I had two big losses around this time. On 29 October 1966, my father, Jack Hewitt, died of a heart attack. He was only 58 years old. Then, very sadly, my grandmother, Emily James, died on 24 July 1967. She brought us up so was very important to us all.

With the girls growing up, I don't know why I would ever consider doing what I did in 1967. I went with my mother and Tony to visit Gerald and Jean to visit Expo 67 in Toronto. This was on the 16th August 1967 and I came back on the 8th September 1967. I have always felt very guilty since then for leaving Valerie on her own with the children. I still do.

It was about 1964/5 when we started our holiday trips to the Toorak Hotel in Torquay and wonderful they were too. I know it was fairly early because on probably our second trip, Sam was around but young and so we left her with Harry and Mattie because we thought the trip was a bit long for a baby. These were annual events every May until about 1974, and included Sam in the ensuing years. We just had a great time and made some great new friends that we kept for many years.

These were also the years of the Potty Pans, Sam's favourite toy*s*.

So, still at Slazenger, in about 1967/8, we moved along by buying a newly-built house – 77 Devonshire Road in Belmont – which again cost a fortune (£5000) but was *detached* this time. Here we made some new friends in the shape Pete and Ena Nattrass who lived just across the road. He was an electrician until he got into his own company and eventually moved to Chicago, where Valerie and I once visited them. Other friends were John and Carol Dean, who I have not heard from in a long time.

We had other friends up and down the street and at one point I used to take the girls with some neighbours' kids to the baths (at Pelton I think) for swimming lessons.

One of my clearest memories of Belmont was Amanda and Sam riding bikes up and down the street. When Amanda first went to school in 1969, on her first day at the Belmont Infants School she went very willingly and seemed to enjoy it. However, the next day when Valerie was getting ready to take her again, she threw a tantrum and said, 'I went yesterday, I don't want to go again!' We got her to school but she hung on to a coat hook and wouldn't let go. It took a while to get her in and on with her education, but it happened eventually.

So, life went on as usual until November 1969 when the new sales manager came after me and made me resign. I was mortified. However, we did have the shop and so was able to lean on that for a day or two when, out of the blue, a guy in Stanley just a few miles away rang me to see if I would like work with him.

And so that is where the next chapter needs to begin since it was a rather pivotal moment.

Chapter 5
White Boot Period

1969 to 1972

November 1969 was the start of a new life away from my roots at Slazenger. It seemed life-threatening to me to be in this position, but within days of leaving Slazenger I was approached by a guy called Alan Westwater who actually knew Gerry from university in Leeds. He also knew me since his family had a small sports shop in Stanley in Count Durham. He had somehow secured the UK rights to sell Hummel Sports footwear and needed some expertise right then. I was a godsend to him at that precise moment. So, luck does play a part in life!

He offered me the job of sales director and matched the Slazenger salary so in economic terms, all was well. Since he was just starting up there was no infrastructure at all - just the potential to import the German-made football boots in time for the following season starting August 1970.

So, the most obvious starting point was for me to take the samples to all my old customers - this included shops around the country that I knew from sports trade shows. So off I went from about January/February 1970 and tried my powers of persuasion out with this new brand.

By about April/May time it became obvious that I wasn't getting far since we didn't have a price advantage with importing from Germany, and Adidas and Puma were so very strong. So we discussed the strategy and I said we needed to come up with something pretty soon which would break the mould and let us in. *No one else has ever been told this,* but I came up with the idea of making WHITE football boots *(which no one in the world had ever done before - they were ALL black)* - and the reason I came up with it was quite simply because the Hummel catalogue from Germany had white hockey boots advertised in it. Those hockey boots looked exactly like football boots. That was it - the only reason I had the idea which then went viral.

So, how to do it?

I just happened to know a chap and his son in Huddersfield who managed two famous footballers: George Best of Manchester United and Alan Ball of Everton. A quick chat with him told us that George was already committed to Stylo footwear, but that Alan was free. We met him and did a deal which I think cost the amazing sum of about £2000 per annum. Imagine that in today's market where they get paid a hundred times that for one week.

We then had to get the prices right by manufacturing in the UK and set up deals with both GB Brittan (TUF Shoes) and the Coop Footwear dept. in Heckmondwyke, near Batley. We put Alan's autograph on the side of the boots, got the samples and off I went again round all my old pals in the trade. This time they laughed at me and asked where the handbags were to go with the white boots. I actually sold only about 3000 pairs before the season was to kick off and we also did not have any boots good enough for Alan to be able to wear. Something had to be done and so we got a pair of his existing Adidas boots and took them to the Coop manufacturer and had them painted white - *several times so they gleamed.*

On 25th August 1970, Everton were playing Chelsea in the first game of the season called the Charity Shield Game. When the players came out onto the field on BBC TV the commentator, Kenneth Wolstenhome, went crazy referring to *Twinkle Toes Alan Ball* all through the match. I took Kenneth out for lunch the following week in Leicester Square to thank him. As a follow up to this, I then signed up a couple of other top line players - Tommy Smith of Liverpool and Charlie George of Arsenal - and put them out in *red* boots - which also went viral.

The rest is pretty much history and to add relevance, between 9am on Monday morning and 12 noon we took orders on the phone for 15,000 pairs. They went ballistic. Especially in Liverpool where the shops couldn't keep up with the sales - and we could not keep up with the orders because we couldn't get them in fast enough.

Alan Ball died a few years ago and when his coffin was set up his white boots were sat on top.

Just for the record as I write this (20th October 2017) I have just been approached again by a writer wanting to do a story on my coming up with this idea.

The business started to grow quickly - probably too quickly – and we added a tennis clothing range. It was then that I first met John Newcombe, the current Wimbledon Champion, and actually got him to model the clothes as a trial. That didn't come to anything but we did remain friends and I saw a lot of him. Valerie and I actually looked after his mum for a day at the next Wimbledon event as she was on her first trip to the UK and he was, of course, tied up playing tennis. I also went out to see him a couple of times at his tennis ranch in New Braunfels Texas and played with him and several other Wimbledon champions. I mostly lost!

One other small story is that whilst still working with Alan Westwater I came up with a new idea, which at the time seemed world changing (remember, no internet or mobile phones). In all the sports shops in the country everyone sold little books from their counters called Know the Game or KTG as it was referred to. These books described all the different sports and how to play them. Since the new systems of the day were things called cassettes which were sound recordings of music on a very small reel to reel which you played on a machine or in your car, I had an idea of turning the KTG book into a recording. At the time (1970), they were in competition with something similar called

8 Track which was slightly different. I got to know a man in Phillips Records in London called Roy Speed who actually came from our area in West Yorkshire somewhere and I told him my idea of putting the KTG information into a sound format via famous sporting stars and they went for it. They invited me to a special private event in their studios to launch a new invention called The Video Player! It was here that I first met Tommy Steele who turned into a lifelong friend.

Amazingly I managed to get a bunch of sports stars together on the basis of commission only and they included John Newcombe for tennis (of course) Jonah Barrington for squash, Henry Cooper for boxing (he invited me to his house for a chat which was nice), someone I can't remember for trampoline, and then a whole bunch (five I think) of footballers who I piled into my car and drove to Manchester where I had organised a studio. They were all famous household names and included Alan Ball and a really famous goalkeeper called Gordon Banks. In today's football world this would be completely impossible without a million pounds in your pocket.

I got the recordings done and then hired a famous presenter from the BBC called John Dunn to be edited in doing the introductions. I took him for lunch and paid him the enormous sum of £25 for his services. He was great and we remained friends for a long time – he sadly died in 2004. I spent a couple of weeks at Phillips Records doing all the final editing in their studios and when they were ready Phillips produced the packaging ready to go to market.

One other little story is about a world trip I made to sell the boots and included a call in Trinidad. The guy I met sent me to see a local major store group with the boots and also sent with me his assistant called Clarence. Clarence was a huge guy and we walked together through a park which was full a people gathered round a band stand on which a man with a megaphone was talking. We walked right under him and just continued out the other side of the park to see the store. On the way back we decided to take the long path back through the park well away from all the speech making and the crowds. But, suddenly, the guy with the megaphone shouted out, 'Invader of the peoples parliament!' With that, all the crowd of people charged towards us shouting and screaming at us like crazy. I said to Clarence to keep moving slowly towards the exit which wasn't far away, to which Clarence said, 'I will kill six of them before they get near us'. It was a very scary moment but fortunately a bunch of policemen came running in and saved us. Phew!

We hired various agents to take on the sales around the country and all seemed well. Except it wasn't, because the balance sheet wasn't working and things were on the verge of going bust in about late 1971 to early 1972. Then there was a fire in the warehouse and office and it all burned down. All was lost, including my Phillips project, and that was the end of Hummel in the UK for that period, and the end of my job too, of course.

However, one really great thing happened during this period. Whilst we were still trying to make the company work, we decided to try and take it to the USA, so both Valerie and I joined

Arnold Robinson (formerly of Slazenger, who now owned Phillips tennis balls) on a trip to San Francisco in September 1971 to a British Week Fair. We both had stands there and Princess Alexandra and Angus Ogilvy did the opening and came to talk

34

to Valerie and myself (there are photos of this as well as a written diary by Audrey Robinson of the visit). The other guy who went on this Frisco trip with Arnold and me was Dave Prowse who was a big-time body builder. When I first met him, he ran the sports department at Harrods, but some time after the trip he became rather famous playing *Darth Vader* in the *Star Wars* films. You never actually saw him because of his metal uniform, but that was him and he is still going around doing it at events around the country. He was in Scarborough last year but unfortunately I missed him. (Editing this in 2022, I hear he's sadly died).

The total trip was amazing and we were there for nearly a fortnight doing trips all over the place. That was the occasion when Valerie and I hired a car and did our wonderful trip to Yosemite Valley. It was fab-u-lous!

Chapter 6

The Yellow Dot Years

1972 to 1981

The '70s was a period of lots of visits to the seaside at Seaham Harbour where we were regularly in the sea. We often had visitors with us such as Valerie's cousin Gillian, and Noel Rigg. Amanda learned to swim very quickly and amazed me by swimming a mile in the baths very early on. Sam started swimming properly a bit later I think but she became better at it than all of us.

Valerie and I used to go to the pictures about once a week in those days and a girl called Zena Tubman used to look after the girls for us. We would usually go to the Metro Centre which was newly built and have pizza first before the film. We actually only had a small pizza between the two of us. We were quite regular visitors to Newcastle to the shops, especially Fenwick's which Valerie loved.

It would be about this time when I joined Durham Archery Tennis Club and started the lifelong friendship with Hugh and Pat Corsie. They were absolutely wonderful and stayed with us through all the years. We went on one American holiday with them through Death Valley, Yuma, Las Vegas and Yosemite Valley and San Francisco, and including a wonderful stop at Apple Farm in San Louis Obispo on the Monterey coast road. It wouldn't be long before we repeated this trip with Sam and a current boyfriend - and Hugh and Pat doing the same journey separately on their own. However, we were forever bumping into them as we went round this enormous country, hardly seemed possible but it did happen.

And so back to business and, having been cut adrift again, I had to come up with a new way to make a living. This next phase was down to a lot of luck in many ways. Firstly, because for some reason squash suddenly came to life in a big way. I had played a bit in the army and again in Durham at the university but nobody could have forecast the growth of the game that was to break out. During the 1970s there were actually about 3 million people playing the game. Today there are only 200,000. (On that basis, my company to be, Yellow Dot, wouldn't have survived).

The success of squash was partly down to a guy called Jonah Barrington who became the world champion and the first person who was actually famous for the sport. I had been making tennis shorts and shirts for the Hummel activity before they fell and the shorts were produced just outside of Bishop Auckland. I met with these guys and got them to make a new style of shorts and make them specifically for the squash market. I then got onto the shirt manufacturer in the midlands and redesigned that by removing the collar. With that I then came up with the name of Yellow Dot simply because of the yellow dot which was on the black squash ball to indicate its speed. I then went to see a friend of Mattie (Valerie's mum) whose son was in the NatWest bank in Sunderland and he arranged for me to have a loan of £4000.

I worked from home to start with and Arnold's wife Audrey (in Nuneaton) did all the invoicing for me until I could afford to get a small office in Durham near the County Hotel. We put all the stock we made into the Bishop Auckland sports shop and got them to do the shipping for us. And, off we went ...

The growth of squash was a boon for Durham, as John Shaw decided to build a squash club in Belmont and this was to provide me with a lot of entertainment and made me into a county level player.

We spent about the first three or four years of Yellow Dot living in Belmont, but as things began to grow and we started to feel a bit on the rich side, we saw a house for sale (newly built) in Darley Court, Plawsworth. It was a bit special, with four bedrooms and cost about £14,000. We had sold the Devonshire Road one for about £9000, so it was quite a climb. I suppose this would be the house that Sam and Amanda would remember most as they were getting on a bit by then.

Val and I took the girls for a holiday in Canada to visit Gerald and Jean on 22 July 1973. We had a great time at Story Book Gardens and Niagara Falls.

By the middle of 1973 Yellow Dot was starting to fly and I was forever off round the world setting up distributors in Australia, New Zealand, South Africa … and ending up with distribution in eighteen countries. In addition to the travelling for sales purposes, I ended up buying shirts and rackets and more from Taiwan and South Korea, as well as other bits and pieces from Hong Kong. This added a lot to my travel and how Valerie put up with me I will never know. We did, however, get trips together to Hong Kong at least once.

By this time we were based in a 6000ft warehouse filled with shelving and with an office. Turnover would have been the equivalent of about £15-20 million in today's money and we employed 50 people including 11 salesmen.

One of the great things we pulled off early in the Yellow Dot years was a deal with British Caledonian Airways (BCAL). This happened simply because we offered them exposure on our brochures in return for them taking us to one of their sunny locations. This went well for some years and also meant that I got to have as many free flights as I wanted for about ten years or so. Val and I used to go to Monaco quite a bit and we also took the girls for a very special holiday in the Seychelles. It was school time and so we had to ask permission to take the girls out. The teacher just said they would learn more on a trip to the Seychelles than they would at school, so we went.

This was one of the great locations which not everyone knew about in those days. It was in about 1978 and we stayed at a hotel called The Reef on Mahe. That was very special and it also introduced me to the manager of a new hotel which was in the process of being built called the Mahe Beach Hotel. This happened because a couple that I knew from Durham happened to have gone to live there (unbeknown to me) and so when I got there they somehow knew about it. He was running the local radio show and asked me to go and be interviewed about sport as they didn't get all that many visitors to the Seychelles in those days. This programme was heard by the Mahe Beach Hotel guy (John Wright) who phoned to ask if we would go and look at his hotel if he sent a car for us? Why not? And he was actually from Huddersfield, West Yorkshire.

Off we went the next day and he ended up putting a squash court in the grounds and I started sending squash coaches out there and organizing squash trips to the hotel from the UK. Due to this, Valerie and I got to go there free with BCAL and stay free at the hotel a few times. Quite a nice arrangement.

I was away a lot in those days, what with setting up and then maintaining contact with those distributors around the world. On these trips I was really lucky to go to two places which were very special. One was my New York agent whose office was high up in the Empire State building with a great view of the East River, and the other was and brilliant place called Century City in Beverley Hills where the hotel looked straight down a road at the end of which there was the hillside with the famous HOLLYWOOD sign on it.

I will never forget one of my very absolute favourite moments when I got back from a trip to Canada and I went with Valerie to collect Sam from school. She came running at me away from her teacher (who was amazed) and literally jumped at me with legs round my waist and arms round my neck crying, "Daddy, my Daddy!" Just like in the film *The Railway Children*. It was amazing.

One of the things that took a lot of time was arranging squash tournaments in the many countries we sold into. We ran these events in each country and then flew all of the winners from each country (courtesy of BCAL) to the Grand Final in San Paolo Brazil. It was quite something *(more on that in the next chapter)*.

It was in September 1975 when we were obviously doing well that we were able to send Amanda and Sam to the Durham High School for Girls which I believe was a great move for them and provided the springboard for what turned out to be their very successful lives. Sam did really well in her early years learning to play the clarinet. So well, in fact, that she ended up playing in a local orchestra which gave concerts all around and which, of course Val and I used to go and see. She still plays a bit today.

There was nearly one tiny hitch to the schooling when, in about 1980/81, I lost Yellow Dot due to it having grown too much and I was unable to fund it properly. Once again, I was bereft of a means of making a living. It was in the summer and it was pretty clear that the private school thing was going to be out of reach, BUT, as ever, something happened quite out of the blue.

I went into the squash club one day and they were just finishing up interviews by ITV for a programme called The Pyramid Game. I had never heard of it. John Shaw the club owner talked the people into interviewing me and guess what? Yes, it was me they picked for the show.

The show actually took place in springtime I think and, amazingly, I won the contest twice, so was on for two weeks (although the shows were recorded straight after one another). I was on with Liza Goddard and a famous guy I can't remember at the moment. So, I won £750 and that paid for the girls to stay on at Durham High. Whoopee!

Other things during this 70-80 period included a famous family trip to Brimham Rocks which is famously recorded on film. This took place in our mobile home which we bought for the company but which was a nice bonus for us personally.

We then went to Oban and the Isle of Mull. I actually wanted to go to the Toorak but Valerie made me turn right and head for Scotland. I sulked a bit on the way up, being a misery guts, but Valerie made me pay for that by giving me the same treatment the following day - all in the spirit of fun. This was probably the only time in our whole lives when we actually had something resembling a fall out. We just never failed to get on. She was perfect in every way.

In the mid-seventies I got back in touch with John Newcombe and Tony Roche who were the Wimbledon doubles champions a few times. I used to collect them from Heathrow Airport and take them straight to Queens Club where we did training together - me providing the service of feeding the balls for them to strike. We used to hit three hundred forehands and then three hundred backhands before stopping for lunch. This relationship put me in touch with a host of other Wimbledon players including Roger Taylor, Bob Hewitt and Frew MacMillan and Fred Stolle.

Late on in the 70s we kept meeting up with Tommy Steele whenever he was playing in local theatres in Newcastle and Sunderland. He used to come back to the house with Val and I. We played squash together quite a lot and used to play for a rusty old trophy called the *Burt Lane Darts Trophy*. Any money we collected went to charity. I also visited Tommy's house in Richmond on a couple of occasions (and met his lovely wife, Anne) and we played tennis on the court in his garden.

Val and I took the girls to see Tommy at the Palladium once and then went round to the stage door to see him and he took us all to his dressing room. Great man and still going. He actually plays tennis at Queens Club where I played every week for several years so we may catch up again. Actually he sent a message to me via a friend of mine at the BBC recently. Very thoughtful of him.

In 1979 I part sponsored a Pro-Celebrity charity event at Queens Club along with the Coral family whom I knew. It was on the middle Sunday of Wimbledon (they didn't play on Sundays back then) and the people who had been knocked out of the Championships used to play at Queens along with various film and TV personalities. I played with Richard Lewis who is now the CEO of Wimbledon and we got to the final and played against Frew McMillan (a Wimbledon doubles champion) and Dustin Hoffman the film star. Dustin and I got on well and we played again after the tournament and he actually invited me to go to New York and stay with him in Greenwich Village where he had an apartment and play tennis at Forrest Hills. I never did that, but I did meet up with him later at his hotel and gave him some Yellow Dot gear.

After the play was finished the whole party then went to a famous night club near Berkeley Square where we (Yellow Dot) put on a fashion show and auctioned the items on show for charity. Quite a nice do.

Also at this tournament was a famous ITV newsreader called Reginald Bosanquet who became a great follower of Yellow Dot (he used to turn up at our fashion shows in London quite frequently). At the Queens Club event he asked me to play for his team which had an annual match against a team from the House of Lords - or was the Commons?

During this period both the girls had piano lessons with the mother of a school friend of Amanda. Amanda continued but Sam gave up but took up the clarinet later. Amanda was also famous about this time for getting to the final of a speaking competition - in German!

Another item from then was the purchase of a horse for Amanda (Sam was completely allergic to them) and I think she got a lot of pleasure out of this for years. I used to ride the horse as well up on Waldridge Fells.

In 1980 Valerie decided she wanted to get further away from other people and we bought a house called Redstacks in Quebec, Co Durham. It was a big old former vicarage with seven bedrooms and two acres of land. We loved it but after exactly a year, the guys from the Guthrie Corporation who were financing Yellow Dot decided to call the money in. Since I couldn't pay them the million that we had outstanding (within a week) they took the company. Served them right though as they hadn't a clue how to run it and they lost everything and had to close it down after less than two years!

Once again on our uppers, we had to sell Redstacks and move into a house a little further down the village. Not perfect but kept us going for a while. That was then the kick-off for the next important phase.

Chapter 7

The Redspot Years
1981 to 1998

1981 and, probably in a fit of annoyance and vengeance, I started up a copycat brand called Redspot. I managed this because of an introduction by a lady I met in Brighton at one our squash events and she introduced me to Martin Wardman. He was actually from around the Bradford area but lived in London and ran an investment business. Just over lunch he offered me whatever money I needed and so we did a deal and off we went.

I worked this from a small office over the Post Office at the top of the hill in Gilesgate - just one or two staff and we soon got into the stride again. At the same time, I kept hold of the tournament activity since we were about halfway through the big event with BCAL of running events in about a dozen countries. Each event produced a winner and those winners would eventually go through to a Grand Final in San Paulo. Because of the loss of Yellow Dot, I had to get a replacement sponsor to run alongside BCAL, and managed to get Dunlop to join in. So on went the event which was to include one of the great moments of my life, as one of the events we had arranged was in Monaco and which, amazingly, allowed me to present the prizes (including the Prince Rainier Trophy) to the winner along with

Prince Albert himself. We got on famously and played tennis afterwards.

The other great thing during this period was pulling in a car rental company (Swan National) for whom we ran an inter-company knock-out squash event all around the UK with a grand final in London. And then THF (Trusthouse Forte) Hotels for around a ten-year period which quite simply meant I always had free cars for my own use (changed for a new one every three months) and that pretty much anywhere we went we flew free with BCAL - picked up our free rental car and then drove to our free hotel. Valerie and I went to Monaco quite often flying into Genoa then driving along the wonderful coast to the Beach Plaza Hotel.

Amanda and Sam both did very well at school and made it to Leeds and Manchester Universities. After that Amanda got her first proper job in Cirencester at a marketing company - all tidy clothes and brief cases. But then Dragoman crossed her path and she ended up being a lorry driver! It was across Africa with tourists, though.

Sam learned more catering skills and went to London working for a cafe chain for a while and staying in a flat just outside Queens Club where I just happened to visit every week on tennis business so got to see her quite often.

Whilst we still had free flights with BCAL, Valerie and I made a trip in the early eighties to Houston Texas, where I went to stay with John Newcombe, three times Wimbledon champion, at his tennis ranch (look it up under Newks Tennis Ranch bit posher now than it used to be but basically the same). Our trip was great. We hired a car and drove around and stayed in San Antonio where The Alamo is located in the centre of town. We went around The Alamo of course but also had a small trip on a canal which runs through the town centre which was awesome. (For the record, the John Wayne film of The Alamo was filmed in a specially built copy of the real Alamo but out of town which is also now a tourist centre. On that trip we stayed in Houston mostly but visited places including Galveston. Weren't we the lucky ones).

At about the same time, I was looking at a companies to help sponsor some of the tournaments I was still running and so got in touch with Cathay Pacific since we had one planned for Hong Kong. They came on board and so we had the flights and then, completely out of the blue, I wrote to Cellnet, who, along with just Vodafone, were starting out in the mobile phone market. Practically no-one had mobiles at that time in the early eighties and so I got a refusal from them.

Amazingly, a few days later a woman phoned me and said they would like to talk about it and a meeting was arranged. They agreed to be the sponsor and that was the start of a long relationship with them and particularly with Paul Leonard. He wasn't actually at Cellnet when I first started with them as he was still working in the parent company BT, however, he came along shortly afterwards and before I knew it they had retained me to handle other things for them in sports sponsorship.

This was actually an amazing period for the whole world, as the introduction of the mobile phone heralded the real start of the computer world that we live in today. Then, the phone battery lasted for about half an hour, at most. At the time I went to London every week to meet up with all my clients including Cellnet and I was literally the only person on the train with a mobile phone. People used to look at me with amazement if I ever used it - which wasn't very often. These London visits went on for some years and I stayed in the lovely Cavendish Hotel (thank you Trusthouse Forte Hotels).

Whilst working for BT Cellnet on sponsorships, we also began a new system on a thing called pager which was the equivalent of today's text messaging. We set up the RACEPAGER which provided all the information on the 'Going

Conditions' and the odds for that day's races anywhere in the country. BT sold millions of them around the UK.

In the early eighties I was approached to do the TV commentary on the British Squash Open at Wembley. Amazing really but it worked okay. Not sure who aired it?

Sadly in April 1981 we lost Valerie's dad, Harry Windrow, known as Poppop. He died in Staincliffe near Dewsbury.

Things were going really well with Redspot by now and in 1983 Valerie and I had seen a house called Biggen Gardens coming to the market and so we sold our house on top of the hill and moved into a rental place just opposite Biggen Gardens so that we could bid for it. It was being sold by a farmer just up the road and we managed to get it for about £40k or so. We then had to spend on it before moving in and Valerie did all the project management. We loved that house and stayed until 1998. This was when Valerie got serious about gardening and she did a great job on things there.

I opened an office in Dragonville, Durham, and started to employ people again as we were fairly well back in business doing sponsorship stuff. I was great at bringing in business and things went well for quite a while, but I was useless at managing people numbers and what they did. I had too many people, paid them too much and never checked what they were all doing. That was my downfall.

During this period, I was going to London for two nights every week and occasionally Valerie would come with me. One of these times was for a dinner to do with sailing, via a friend who was a director of Lillywhites in Piccadilly. Dick and Margo Harle went with us on this one and the great moment for Valerie was that Bernard Cribbens was there (*of The Railway Children fame*) so she just went straight across the room and asked him to dance. How could he refuse?

In 1988 we had been married 25 years and Valerie gave me a wonderful letter which, of course, I still have today.

The following year was my 50th birthday and Valerie and the girls arranged a special party for me. This entailed getting me to play squash with Dr Geoff Madison (who sadly died in early 2025) in the afternoon whilst all the visitors from far and wide gathered together up in the bar area and I was trapped. All these great people came and were introduced gradually and Amanda had arranged for it all to be filmed (we all have a copy).

In 1985 I managed to get a meeting in Luton with Vauxhall Motors. I asked them to sponsor a squash event I had dreamed up and a great man who became a good friend - *Alan MacKay* - said no to that - but could I do anything in tennis? Quick answer to that was YES! I didn't have a plan at the time but soon dreamed one up.

That took us into a great period of about ten years where we ran the event called the *Indoor Tennis Trophy*. The reason for this was that it was just about that time that indoor tennis centres had just started to open around the country. The event consisted of teams of four from every club in the UK playing singles and doubles. It started with all the teams in eight areas of the country competing to go into the final eight (quarter finals) and then playing off to establish the final pair who played for the trophy and a prize of £40,000. This went really well and we even got the final shown on Channel 4 television one year - with me commentating!

A small anecdote about the Vauxhall Motors event was that I took on a young woman called Sarah Clarke (her first job) and trained her on the running of the event which she then took over and did very well prior to leaving a few years later to join the Lawn Tennis Association. She eventually went on to join government and, in 2018, became the first ever female Black Rod.

During the period of 1990 I did get another go at broadcasting by doing a test as a Wimbledon commentator at the BBC TV Centre but they failed to give me the job.

So, I tried another trick and wrote directly to the Director General of the BBC and suggested that I might be good at this stuff and could I see him. The rule for the BBC is that since we are his employer (as license fee payers) he is bound to reply. This he did and said that my enquiry had been sent to an Anthony Cherry - who was currently producing a TV show with David

Jacobs called *Primetime*. This was an afternoon show for older people, run like a tea dance. Anthony was good enough to phone me to ask what experience I had. Obviously, I had to say that I did not have any experience. His response to that was that he was approached every week by about 25 people who *did* have experience so my chances were nil.

Never say die, I said that I was in London every week and would he have lunch with me at Grosvenor House? He said yes and that was that. We had great rapport and he ended it by saying that he would organise a screen test for me. This he did along with a six-man camera crew at Eton College.

Following that he gave me the job on Primetime of being the active person who would go out with famous people to show that even at 50 one could still do things. My first job was going to be skating with Torvill and Dean apparently.

I went to the first production meeting along with David Jacobs and the other stars and producers where we discussed what was going to happen.

But then, literally just a few days later, a senior lady executive producer was suddenly free from the Ester Rantzen show and she was put in charge of *Primetime* over Anthony and his partner producer. She apparently decided to do my role as a voice-over rather than an action man type of thing, so that was me out. I tried the same trick with the new lady of lunch at Grosvenor House but I couldn't change her mind so that was that, my stardom was over before it had begun.

The great win out of all this was that Anthony and I became the very best of friends and still are to this day. Also, Anthony introduced me to Gloria Hunniford, who is still broadcasting today. It turned out that she wanted to become a member of Queens Club where I played every week. Sadly she couldn't get in as there was a seven year waiting list. Well, me being me, I had the inside track at Queens and so just spoke to the manager there and persuaded him to allow Gloria to become a member.

She was over the moon and we became friends for a while. She was very nice.

In January 1992 we very sadly lost Val's mum, Beatrice Martha Windrow (Mattie). She had moved up to Durham where we had bought her a house in Langley Park so she ended her life close to Valerie.

With Mattie's house being free, we then invited my mother Lucy to come and live there as she had fallen once or twice at her house in Birstall. She came up for a while but, not that I knew this at the time, she didn't like it and so she found a place near Blackpool (Starr Hills Methodist Home) which turned out to be really lovely. She moved there in July 1996 and was happy there until she died peacefully on 6th January 2003.

Somewhere around this point in time, Sam decided to leave the catering business and come back home. So, she came to work with me and set up a mobile phone shop in the office. This was the early days of the mobile phone and with hindsight I think if we had worked on that and stayed with it we might have ended up as Carphone Warehouse. Or perhaps not!

Around 1994, I was asked by Trusthouse Forte Hotels if I would like to take on the management of the Leisure Centre at the De La Bere Hotel in Cheltenham. Seemed like a good idea and so I did that, and in the end Sam went down there to help manage it. Good move as that is why she and Tim, her now husband, met.

Better news later in 1992 with Amanda setting out on married life with Guy, and 1997 Samantha followed suit with Tim. Both turned out to be excellent choices and they are just wonderful

partnerships. The weddings were really nice and both receptions were held at Lambton Castle in Chester-le-Street. To say both couples worked well together is an understatement as they each work together in their respective businesses. There can be few marriages as good these two anywhere in the world and I will always be grateful to the boys for being so great.

One of the great moments of our life was that I bought a number of trophies for the Vauxhall event from Tiffany's. I got to know the lady there and she was a riding companion of Princess Diana.
    Whilst talking with her one day, I mentioned *Breakfast at Tiffany's* being the meeting point for Valeria and me, and Moon

River our special song. She said, "Would you like to bring her for breakfast at Tiffany's one day?" Would I?!

I planned the date and surreptitiously took Valerie to London on some pretext and suggested that we go out for breakfast the next morning. We walked up Bond Street and, of course, stopped to look in Tiffany's window, just like Audrey Hepburn. This was fairly early morning before the store was open but a man in a smart green uniform was standing outside and suddenly came up to us, saluted and said, "Mr and Mrs Hewitt, would you like to come this way please?"

Can you imagine Valerie's amazement? We went in and were taken up to the office area where a table was laid for breakfast with champagne! Another couple joined us and we were served by the management. It was completely unbelievable and when we had finished, we were given the run of the shop before it was opened up to the public and it was when I bought Valerie a silver necklace with a jug on it. I got lots of brownie points that day and we remain two of only a very small handful of people in the world who have done that. I went in not too long ago and asked about it and they no longer do it.

Val's cousin, Gillian, and her husband, Barry, did a lovely thing for us on Valerie's birthday (Gillian thought it was her 60th but in fact it was her 59th). They arranged for us all to go to their house in Barbados. Valerie thought it was just us as we flew alone, but when we arrived Amanda and Sam and the boys were waiting there. Valerie was so shocked that she almost fell over, but I was behind and held her up.

One small interesting little aside came about via a small film which was made by the International Tennis Federation showing a couple of Land Rovers carrying tennis players into remote areas of Africa and taking tennis into the villages. Once there, they set up a small court with a piece of rope replacing the net and the kids using wooden bats which they had made in the woodwork lessons prior to the visit. The execs of ITF explained to me that whilst it was good to be able to take tennis out there it was sad that the kids went back to playing with pebbles once the team left as they could not get nor afford tennis balls.

My reaction was that it was a shame that all these balls used in the UK for just a few games were then being replaced (Wimbledon use 3000 dozen in the fortnight) and lost forever. This brought me an idea which was to get sponsors and make up boxes to be sent to every club in the UK so that all used balls could be saved and collected for the deprived kids. We called it Bank a Ball.

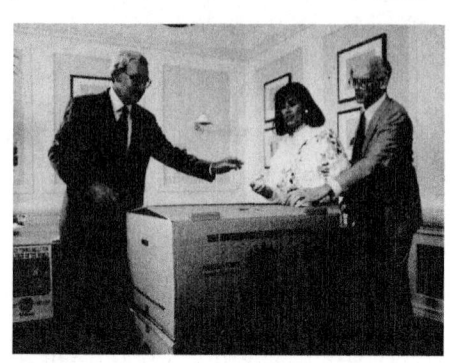

The two main sponsors were Bowater Scott (as they were called then) who made the boxes, and Parcel Force who would deliver the empty boxes to the clubs and then collect them again when they were full. In addition, we had support from Wilson Sporting Goods who provided us with Wimbledon Champion Stefan Edberg to front the operation. From there I got an airline to deliver the balls all over the world to the deprived kids. We actually managed to collect around 1 million balls! So quite a result. The ITF said they would give me 10 cents for each ball collected but they never got round to it.

The next three years went along with in the same style but then started to slow down for two main reasons. First was that my Vauxhall contacts - Alan MacKay in charge of sponsorship retired and the Chairman Bill Ebbert with whom I played tennis at Queens Club every Wednesday night was posted back to the

USA. So, I lost my main connection and with it the event and the income.

In 1998 BT sold Cellnet to a Spanish company and, although I stayed in touch with BT for a while, it was basically over for the two biggest income streams I had been living with. Instead of downsizing and getting rid of people, I just tried to replace the business and ended up out of business.

Chapter 8

Back to Yorkshire
1998 to early 200s

Valerie decided that she would like to move down to Yorkshire. We looked at a number of houses before coming across Wiganthorpe - via Christine Horne - and we moved there. The move back to Yorkshire was precipitated by the final failure of my business empire, such as it was. I was pretty good at ideas and setting things off, but useless at managing them.

After losing everything (again) it was absolutely amazing that Barry Rubery, Gillian's husband (who was vastly better at business than me) offered to buy our next house and let us live in it for the rest of our lives. There are not many like him around.

It was August 1998, and I was back to my starting place of Yorkshire, though living somewhere slightly posher than Batley. Our house at Wiganthorpe was newly built and part of a group developed from farm buildings. Valerie quickly licked it into shape and the area was very nice with quick access to the coast at Scarborough, Filey and Whitby.

I still went to London regularly and did small bits of business along with Paul Leonard but nothing serious. In 1999/2000 Barry bought Huddersfield Football Club and he asked me to set up his commercial department. I went there for a couple of years whilst still doing my own stuff. He got out a bit later.

I had another lovely meeting whilst at the club: I met Delia Smith who owned Norwich Football Club. We got on well and arranged to meet for lunch at Langhans Brasserie in London. We met there a few times along with her husband Michael Wynn-Jones and once she knew about Amanda living just down the road in Suffolk, invited us both to lunch at her house. It was in the house where the BBC used to film her cooking programmes. That was a bit special.

It was in Bishop Burton college that Valerie started to make great inroads with her gardening expertise. She made some good friends there and went on to win a *Bronze Medal* at the Harrogate Flower Show. Pretty good! Of course, she made our own garden absolutely wonderful.

In this next period we had visits from both Gerry and Joan from Canada and they both had to put up with visits to Morecambe and Blackpool for their sins. Valerie and I made two trips to Barry and Gillian's house in Barbados as well as Valerie making a trip to Egypt with Gillian.

Things continued until the moment we went with Amanda and Guy to Egypt to celebrate our Ruby Wedding anniversary year. On 28th September, this ended in the worst of all possible ways. Valerie was thrown from her camel and thus ended the life of one of the best people who ever existed. She died in Cairo hospital on 9th October 2003.

Prior to this trip Amanda and Guy had started the process to adopt two children which then had to be put on hold for a while thus denying Valerie the chance of ever seeing either Luke or Dan. Very sad for all parties.

So, that was the end of life as I knew it and where my head was I have no idea. I think when I met with people I tried to act normally but the moment I was alone I fell apart and life was appalling.

Fortunately for me we had met a few people who were walking buddies with Pat and Hugh. One of these was Maureen Bean whom we had therefore known for quite a lot of years. We went out to the cinema a couple of times and became very good friends and spent weekends together. Maureen had a stroke along the way and she came and stayed with me so I could look after her through the week. And this went on until we decided to make it permanent by selling her house. It was the stability she brought to my life at that difficult time that probably saved my life - it probably wasn't easy for Mo having known Valerie and how close we had been, but she coped amazingly - and still does!

Mo and I did a really amazing thing together in planning a trip to Alaska and the west coast for a month. The Alaska part of the trip was on a small fishing boat and was one of the great experiences of all time. Tagged on the end of the cruise was a three-week drive around the Canadian Rockies which was out of this world.

Life started to get back to something like normal and I started a website for Sponsorfinder which Tim made for me. I also restarted going to London each week and linking up with Paul Leonard and Simon Ingman who had both retired from BT. We did a few small things which provided some interest but achieved very little on the financial front.

I also kept up my connection with Anthony Cherry at the BBC which has always been one of my favourite things - a really terrific person.

I maintained a connection with Durham in that I stayed with my dentist of 50 years or so and also via Stephen Squirrell my accountant. We also had a close tie with Pat and Hugh Corsie, of course, and saw them quite often.

On the home front, we did look around at moving into a new house so that Mo could feel it was *hers* - a feeling which was quite understandable. We went all over the place including Morecambe, would you believe!

In the end we found nothing that made us want to leave Wiganthorpe and so we settled down here.

So that's it. From Batley to Wiganthorpe (via Durham and some incredible experiences), with love.

An Additional Chapter

Daughters' Perspectives

Early 2019

You inevitably grow up with only patchy knowledge of your parents' lives. You've heard a lot of stories over the years, you think you know them better than most people (and you do in many ways), but actually you always know them as Mum or Dad and, important as that is, it's only one side of who they are.

I'm so pleased you wrote this memoir, Dad, but, as you reach the respectable age of 80, Sam and I wanted to write some words of our own as an added chapter in your life story.

From Amanda

I don't remember never sleeping at night. I don't remember long periods of Dad being away (some, yes, but not lots). I don't remember not wanting to go to school on the second day (though I feel like I do, as I've heard the story many times!).

I *do* remember always being totally loved. I still do. Mum and Dad gave me the strongest foundation any parent can give a child: they loved me, believed in me, backed me, encouraged me, and yet didn't try to hold on too tightly. I had freedom to make mistakes and explore life.

As a mum myself now, I can imagine that when I went out for the first few times on Nutmeg, my horse, their hearts were probably in their mouth. I should think that when I decided to become an overland leader and drove across Africa, they were constantly wondering if I was OK, since there was no contact for weeks/months on end.

Dad was always a joy to be around. He was always fun and willing to play or take us to the beach or whatever. Sam and I knew he was a soft touch, but I'm not aware of taking advantage of that (maybe we did!?). I really don't remember Dad ever getting cross; we knew that Mum was the rule-maker and -enforcer in the house. We, mostly, did as we were told — and so did Dad!

But that doesn't mean Mum was super strict; she wasn't. She just wanted things how she wanted them as we were growing up. She was always there for us, always loved us, and did everything in her (considerable) power to give us a good life and bring us up well.

The other thing that Mum did was to love Dad — totally, wholeheartedly, without reservation. And the same was true of Dad — he adored Mum.

Living in a house where there is no doubt at all that each person is worthy of being loved, whatever, is an incredible gift to have been given.

Snapshots of Dad from Amanda

- Coming home and going to sleep on the settee before dinner, covered up in a newspaper, and occasionally accompanied by a dog (Prudy, our English setter, in the early days at Darley Court) or a cat (Tiger was our first cat).
- Playing the piano. Which got me and Sam interested too.
- Absolutely loving his food!
- Constantly playing squash or tennis, and getting into trouble from Mum for leaving sweaty clothes lying around!

- Making any of my friends that came to visit feel welcome and making them laugh, as he does with many people.
- Always talking to strangers when we were out and about, especially in restaurants where he loved asking them to pay his bill. Sam and I were shown that anyone and everyone is worth talking to and getting to know.
- Wearing embarrassingly bright trousers sometimes.
- Teaching us to play squash and tennis. We loved going to the squash club with Dad, and even hanging around waiting for him to have a game afterwards because we got crisps and pop at the bar.
- Going to Seaham beach on Sunday mornings while Mum stayed home to cook Sunday lunch.
- Often forgetting to pick us up from High School! Funnily enough, we didn't mind, we just thought, 'Oh Dad's forgotten us again. He'll realise soon.'
- Teaching us to swim and ride a bike.
- Bringing Foxy Loxy (a big red and black soft toy almost as tall as me, with elastic on his feet so you could dance with him!), a moccasin necklace (wish I still had that) and other presents back from abroad.
- Loving cowboy movies and James Bond.
- Going to the Seychelles and Canada and Monte Carlo, and Dad being super excited about it all, which was very infectious.
- Seeing Mum and Dad going out to parties etc, and thinking they were the very glamorous (especially Mum).

- Being very proud of Mum and Dad, and always feeling that no-one could possibly have better parents than mine. I felt privileged.

Memories from Sam

What a fabulous life we have had. We've seen all corners of the earth and experienced life to the full, with the most amazing parents. Who needs money when you have been loved and cared for in the way we both have and continue to be? Dad is the richest man on earth with the biggest heart and I couldn't be more proud to call him *my* dad. How lucky am I!

- Cleaning teeth 3x a day. I always thought it was a bit excessive but I do that now!
- Great cooked breakfasts
- DIY expert … not. I seem to recollect him changing a lightbulb or something in Darley Court and the whole ceiling coming down!
- Crying at soppy films.
- *Ice Cold In Alex* film. One of his favourites but I never did get the story and it was so boring.
- Flying Peter Powell kites on Waldridge Fell.
- Being in Tommy Steele's dressing room.
- On holiday in Spain, Dad cleaned everything with Dettol.
- Playing Swing Ball
- Carving the sirloin of beef for Sunday dinner

- Rice pudding, jam roly poly …
- Dad always had Weetabix and hot milk years ago for breakfast. I hated the smell of it and it was all soppy. Yuk
- Mum and Dad queued up at the music shop in Newcastle really early to buy me my first clarinet which was in a great sale (Elkhart). They always took me everywhere to participate in the Durham show band (Mr Scholard) and Northern youth orchestra. I had Mr Robinson for lessons.
- Pink wine and tonic!
- At Dad's 50th he kept saying 'Me and Hughie are 101 today'.
- Great memory lane trip with Dad visiting all our old houses, schools, Seaham, Windrow sports shop, then a fab meal at the Black Bull to top a fabulous day with me Dad.
- Dad holding me and Mand up in the sea in Seychelles, one in each hand, as the waves crashed around us
- The Toorak: grab machine, double ended swing, boiled eggs with knitted hats, magnolia tree …
- Dad taking cover on the swing at Darley Court as Mum dealt with the mouse behind the washing machine.
- Draper of Glastonbury suede slippers. They have been there our whole life in various colours.
- Never wearing new clothes until they've hung in the wardrobe for at least 2 years!
- Saving me from several jobs: failing at the Heathrow T4 hotel, Dad sent me on a 6-month overland across Africa with Mand at the helm; failing in London Richoux restaurant, Dad gave me a job at BH Associates as a

telephone sales person and then sent me to the De La Bere Hotel to run the bar and eventually meet the love of my life.

- When Tim asked Dad if he could have his permission to ask me to marry him, he saw the great relief on Dad's face!

And a final word from the editor!

As I grew older and left home, I found that I loved exploring the world, however, I've always wanted to go back home regularly too. I always wanted to be sure that Mum and Dad were healthy and happy (which they always were), and that we kept the strong bond we have. We did.

When Mum died, the world was rocked for Sam and I, and we struggled to come to terms with her loss for quite a long time. But, of course, this was nothing to how it affected Dad. Sam and I were so worried about him. We really didn't know how he would cope – if he would cope.

And this came on top of Guy and I trying to adopt our boys, and indeed, going on to adopt them 6 months after Mum's death. Looking back, it was a hell of a time; partly horrendous (added to by Sam's car accident), partly joyous. Life certainly keeps us on our toes.

I still wonder how things would have panned out if Mo hadn't come into our lives. I'm convinced it would have been far, far more difficult.

Mo is a remarkable woman and thank goodness Dad recognised that. I know relationships are always a two-way street, but from my point of view, Mo came and loved and cared for Dad at a time when I wasn't sure how he was going to ever be happy again. Since she knew and loved Mum, I'm sure Mo knew she was taking on a rather difficult role initially, but she did it sensitively and very well. Not only that, but she didn't even hesitate to take on the role of grandma (though she's always been known as Mo) for the boys. Dad picked well, again!

Dad, you have the enviable knack of making people happy. We are aware that you feel you've not succeeded in some ways in your life — you never made your million (yet!) — but to us that is a small thing, an unimportant trifle.

Having a happy life without causing suffering to anyone or anything else is surely one of the main things we are all striving to do, and anyone who adds happiness to this world is a blessing.

Dad, you make us happy.

Lots of love always,
from your girls,
Amanda and Sam xxx

With Pat and Hugh Corsie

Printed in Dunstable, United Kingdom